My Beard Will Do The Trick

And Other Poems

Ganesh Eashwar

BookLeaf
Publishing
India | USA | UK

Made with ❤ on the BookLeaf Publishing Platform
www.bookleafpub.in
www.bookleafpub.com

Dedication

Dedicated to everyone I came across,

I met, I loved, I hated, I aped...

After all...

No poet, no writer,

would write as much

as he did,

if a poet, a writer,

wrote only what he did.

What he experienced!

A poet, a writer,

often writes

what he imagines he did.

A poet, a writer,

often writes what his friends did,

he wishes he had.

Or hadn't.

Every poet, every writer,

revels in flights of imagination.

Acknowledgement

Thanks to all the help I received from family, friends and associates over the years - each helped in their own individual way, and as much as they could each do, comfortably. Of course, I took care not to demand more than I thought was fair.

Thanks, alphabetically, Ajit, Amitabh, Anita, Boozie, Daddy, Deepi, Jag, Jeje, Lalli, Manasi, Manu, Meena, Meenakshi, Mummy, Nasty, Nidhi, Nikhil, Parmesh, Paul, PJ, Pradeep, Prashant, Savi, Sharath, Snegha, Usha, Vaaru...

And the poets, readers and admins at Allpoetry.com and Kavishala.com.

Cover Design: GE Featherstonehaugh
Author's Cover Photo: Manasi Jagdish

Preface

In this, my first short collection of poems to be published, I've chosen to share a range of my poems, rather than follow a theme, or choose my favourites. A co-poet and a contest host on Allpoetry.com had commented "You seem capable of writing about anything." Felt good.

So, come with me on a roller coaster ride - albeit a gentle one! You'll get to read - here and in my future books - about birth, death, love, hate, politics, spirituality, nature... And some pure whimsy.

I write what I write
Wrong or right.
Love vs lust
Hurt or trust.
Religion vs politics
Strategy or tactics.
Street smarts vs college degree
Medicine vs quackery.

Online or in ink
I write what I think.

My Beard Will Do The Trick

As we
grow older
and begin
to regress
to our childhood,
skipping
the golden years
of our youth

We'll need
help
sitting up,
standing,
walking,
talking,
getting
into bed...

We'll need
diapers,
strollers,

push chairs...
But, one thing
I won't need
is a bib
when I'm being fed.

My beard
Will do
the trick,
instead.

My Beard Gets in the Way

These days
my long beard
gets
in the way
of my
shirt buttons,
winter jacket zips,
my specs on a string...

Those days,
their long hair
never got
in the way
of zippering down
their gowns,
or unclasping
their bras...

How?
I wonder,
these days!

Mother

I have had
the privilege
of staying
in Palace Hotels,
in run-down Motels,
in B&Bs,
and under the sky.

I have had
the privilege
of staying
in cities,
in towns,
in districts,
and in villages.

I have had
the privilege
of staying
in bungalows,
in apartments,
in cottages,
and in huts.

I have had
the privilege
of staying
in self-owned premises,
in company-leased properties,
in rented accommodation,
and with friends and relatives.

I even had
the privilege
of staying
in a place
with free
board and lodging.
No EMI. No rent.

Just once.
For nine months.

Thank you, Mother.

Don't Feel Bad, Dad

I know Dad,
you both laboured
most of your lives
to grow me, to groom me.

But don't feel bad, Dad,
even for a moment,
if I give more credit
to her, than to you.

She laboured nine months
to produce me.
You laboured seven minutes,
lay back contentedly.

Don't feel bad, Dad
I fully understand.
For I, too, am
just a mere dad.

The Business Of War

War is never
between two peoples.
Always between
two rulers,
two governments,
two bullies,
two idiots.

Arms akimbo
each will talk
to his lieutenants,
in heroic aggression,
egging on his soldiers
from the safety
of his office,
his special bunker,
his lady's boudoir,
to kill, kill, kill.

Many soldiers
will die,
many women

will be widowed,
many parents
bereft of their child,
many children
bereft of their parents.
But the leaders
the weapon makers,
the toadies,
and the cronies,
will make a neat killing.
On both sides.

What a lucrative business, war is!

The Itchy Finger

Nations
have used
individual
acts of guts
and bravado
to romanticise war.

Victors
and losers
valorise
individual heroics
to up their cause
and launder their ills

Today
Putins and Netanyahus
need no such heroes
nor heroics.
Just some
innocuous buttons.

And a suitably itchy finger!

Sunday Indolence

It's a Sunday afternoon
my pillows and my bed
compete coquettishly.
The bed promises
to envelope me
in its softness.
The pillows wink
they'd be happy
just to feel
the comfort of my head
on their bosom!

I accept
the inevitable...
A threesome!

But, how I wish you were here.

The Pillow

The squishy warmth of a pillow,
matched only by a mother's embrace,
or the early morning glow.

But, mothers can become stern,
the sun can burn,
pillows share unwavering warmth.

I Write About Death
Not Unfrequently

Paul worries
that I write
about death
not unfrequently.

But I write
as frequently
about life
about love
about hate
about growing up
about growing old
about pleasure
about pain
about today
about yesterday
about tomorrow...

I am no escapist.
Nor afraid of death.

Death is not
my dominant concern.
It is not even a concern.
Merely an awareness.
So, I write
about death.

I worry
about death
like I worry
about
whether the house
is properly locked up,
the iron
switched off,
the cooking gas
turned off,
just as we head out
on a long-awaited holiday.

I write
about death
like I would write
a will,
while

still enjoying all
I've bought
and got.

I write
about death
like I'd write
about spring cleaning,
like getting rid
of the unnecessary,
like sorting out
the huge collection
of memorabilia
of clothes
of papers
of junk...

Leaving some
with people
to enjoy,
leaving others
safely hidden
from prying eyes,
while I'll be gone
on this eternal holiday.

Who Will I Be Thirty Years From Now

An enthusiastic speck
of fine, fine ash.

Dead.
But not buried.
Cremated.
Burnt.
To a cinder.
A speck.

But,
a speck
looking,
searching,
hunting
for other specks
I may have known.

Hoping
to recognise...
Family.

Friends.
Neighbours.
Acquaintances.
Employers.
Employees.
Associates.
Anyone.

Not a lost soul.
Not a restless soul.
Just an eager one.

An enthusiastic speck
of fine, fine ash.

The Erogenous Ear

If I were
a Doctor,
if I were
your Doctor,
I'd never ever
need a stethoscope,
I'd never ever
use a stethoscope,
when
thine nipple
so snugly
fits mine ear.

Pardon Me, Lady

Every time
I am with you
my heart
goes haywire!

Since I dance
to the drumbeat
of my heart,
so does my dancing.

So,
pardon me,
Lady.
Did I step on your toes?

His Gentle Touch

His hand
had for decades,
reached around,
in the middle
of the night,
to reassure himself
she was still there.

And well.

That gentle touch
had for decades,
reassured her,
in the middle
of the night,
he was well
and looking out for her.

No matter
what idiocies
he'd been up to,
during the day.

But, one day,
both knew,
his hand would fail
to reach around to find her.

Or, one day
both knew,
his hand would reach around
and find her not there.

Which would happen?
Each thought about it.
Never discussed it.

Both lived in the moment.

Eloquence

Why
do your eyes
and your face
talk a different
language?

I learn one,
only to find
the other
has got
more eloquent.

And worse,
your tongue
translates
them both
oh, so wrong.

Can't we
just let
our hands
and bodies
do the talking?

They
understand
each other.
Speak
a universal language.

Eloquently.

A Vintner I May Be

Maybe
I am not
A bad winemaker.

Even as my body
Is turning
Into vinegar.

My mind
Is turning
To great wine.

How Many Seeds

In my childhood
our grandmother
taught us
counting.
Using the seeds
of pomegranates.

That habit
hasn't died.
Not yet!
I still count
while eating
a pomegranate:

How many teeth remaining?

We Sit At Waitered Tables

We sit
at waitered tables
scrupulously
picking out food
we think
ought to be
garbage.

They sit
at garbage dumps
scrupulously
picking out garbage
they think
could do as
food.

The Size Of The Cake?
Or The Size Of The
Slice?

In stadiums and public parks,
in self-congratulatory words,
many a leader drones on, about how
under their watch, the GDP has grown!

But, I can't take my eyes off
the old man, around a dustbin,
gathering food off the ground.
Food other people have thrown.

Even a child knows well,
that the size of the cake
is not as important
as the slice each is given.

When will our leaders ever learn?

On A 16th Floor Balcony

Wistfully, she leaned
on the balustrade
16 storeys high
braving her fear
of heights
and the Madras Sun.

Mesmerised
by the ever busy waters
she watched
the Bay of Bengal
capriciously change
its colours from time to time.

She'd lived a lifetime in Madras
yet never tired of the sea.
It beckoned her always.
Often relentlessly:
"Come, come with me
to magical shores!"

She stood there
unmindful of

the sun above,
the vultures around,
and inside
beseeching grandchildren.

Wondering...
If I could walk down
just 16 flights of stairs,
could I walk the ocean floor?
Under the waters of the Bay?
To shores far away?

And she allowed
a solitary, salty tear
to make its desperate way
down her cheek
hoping to meet the sea
down below.

The New Antique

Jayashree, my wife,
was a keen collector
of antiques,
even before we first met.

She added
more & more,
over the years,
to her eclectic hoard.

Today, as I stood
staring into the mirror,
birthday reminiscing,
it hit me with a thud...

Eerily prescient,
Jayashree could
spot an antique
yet to be.

And there in the mirror
staring back at me,
was one she'd picked up

way back in 1973.

And Lord Rama Whispered To Sita...

Bemused
by all the fanfare,
Lord Rama
arrived in Ayodhya
ahead of Inauguration Day...

With just a glance
he took in all -
his new abode,
the food for invitees,
the ostentation of lights...

Whispered to Sita:
"This is not for me...
This mandir. This show...
It's for them,
and their elections...

"I need
no home
no house

no palace
no mandir...

"I need
no prasad
no food
no chai
no coffee...

"I need
no diyas
no candles
no lights
no ostentation...

"Let them
light up
the lives
of the poor.
That's enough for me.

"Let them
give the poor
enough food
each day.

That's enough for me.

"Let them
give me
a little space
in their hearts.
That's enough for me.

"I'll make my home in there."